This book is dedicated to the Lace Guild
which was formed in 1976
to promote all forms of lace.

It is hoped that all its members
who are lucky enough to acquire old lace
or make new lace
will treasure and preserve it for the future
as Elsie Turnham did during her lifetime.

This is copy no

73
....

of a special edition
of five hundred signed copies

The Turnham Family

Elsie Turnham
Lace Collector

The Story of Bucks Point Lace
and the
Elsie Turnham Lace Collection

Diana J Adams

Diana J. Adams

E. Mary Adams

Designed by Peter Tucker, typeset in Bembo
and printed at the Alden Press, Oxford

The Kylin Press, Darbonne House, Waddesdon, Buckinghamshire

ISBN 0 907128 17 3

Contents

HENRY TURNHAM,

Foreword

My aunt, Elsie Turnham, was born in Waddesdon, Buckinghamshire, on June 5th, 1885. Her father and my grandfather, Henry Turnham, was the proprietor of The Marlborough Arms.

The Marlborough Arms in Waddesdon High Street

Over many years, she amassed a unique collection of lace and working tools from the traditional Bucks lace makers at a time when bobbins and straw pillows (with their wooden *'horses'*) were being burnt or thrown away.

Towards the end of her life, living in the County Town of Aylesbury, she deeply regretted that the well-known centres of lace making – such as Olney and Newport Pagnell – were portrayed as producing superior quality work. This had not been her own experience as she recalled:

"I found in my visits to old lace makers many proofs of equally fine lace and I have some fine specimens and parchments equal to any illustrations or exhibits I have ever seen."

Today, amidst a major revival of interest in lace making, my sister and I are placing the *'Elsie Turnham Collection'* on exhibition to show local examples of this once extensive *'cottage industry'* and to illustrate the importance of the Vale of Aylesbury as a centre of fine lace. But most of all we hope that Elsie Turnham's efforts will help to encourage today's revival of interest in producing fine lace.

Lace Making

Lace has gone through many stages of transition to produce the lace we collect and make today and more than one European country claims to have been the originator of *Bobbin Lace*. However it is generally accepted that the Flemish refugees from religious persecution brought *Bobbin Lace* to England and particularly to the East Midlands.

It is fascinating to think that these early refugees would have brought with them their lace pillows. After all they were fleeing for their lives, on foot, and yet they took with them their most prized possessions – their lace making equipment. No wonder that, as soon as they were given shelter and had the rudiments of a home again, they started to work their lace. They must have been very similar *'country folk'* to those living in Bedfordshire and Bucks: the landscape was similar and so, no doubt,

Lace makers at Maids Moreton near Buckingham

was their way of life, with the men working in the fields and the women in the cottages.

The first straw-filled pillows were bolster shaped and more than likely made by the village saddler by ramming straw tightly into a cloth bag to form the foundation, just as he made the big collars worn by the cart and plough horses.

The countryside had available all materials for lace making equipment and the men would carve the pillow-horses from woods in the hedgerow and

Saddlers at work in Waddesdon

the bobbins from the wood of the fruit trees in the garden. This *'cottage industry'* meant that these women, could *'work at lace'* in their own homes and quite often could earn more than the agricultural worker on the land.

This pattern was repeated in villages throughout Buckinghamshire. In Sheahan's *'History of Bucks'*, published in 1862, the following places are mentioned as being engaged in the trade:

"Bierton (black and white lace)*; Cuddington; Haddenham; Great Hampden; Wendover; Gawcott* (black)*; Beachampton; Marsh Gibbon; Preston Bissett; Claydon; Grendon; Dorton; Granborough; Oving* (black and white)*; Waddesdon; Newport Pagnell;*

Five lace makers of Waddesdon just before the First World War

Bletchley; Hopton; Great Horwood; Bow; Brickhill; Fenny Stratford; Hanslope (where 500 women and children are employed, about one-third of the population)*; Lavendon; Great Sandford, Loughton; Milton Keynes; Moulsoe, Newton Blossomville, Olney; Sherrington;* and the adjoining villages, *Stoke Hammond, Wavendon; Great and Little Kimble; Wooleston, Aston Abbots, Swanbourne, Winslow, Radnage,* etc."

Waddesdon was one such *'lace'* village. Silk was also manufactured in the village and today there is still a *Silk* Street, but alas it has no *Lace* Street.

For centuries Waddesdon was an agricultural village, like so many more in Buckinghamshire. With over 100 cottages each with a big family, there was no employment for the wives or children except on the land or in the farmhouses or dairies. There were a dozen or so farms of between 300 to 400 acres, each employing from five to ten agricultural workers living either in tied cottages, in the village itself, or near the farms.

The 1881 census for Waddesdon shows one boy of eight as a *'lace maker'* – perhaps he ought to have been a *'scholar'*! Another entry shows a female of fifteen as *'head of household'* and several younger brothers and sisters as *'lace makers'*. Children were sent to lace schools where they were taught by rule of thumb or, if their parents could not afford the minimal fee, by picking it up at home watching

Waddesdon High Street, circa 1880

Baker Street, Waddesdon

their mothers or grandmothers. One could hardly blame a child for sneaking out of school where she was expected to make complex *Point Lace* before she had made the easier kinds of *Braid Lace*. One important benefit might be an opportunity to learn to *'read and write'* as the Vicar's wife might attend to read to the pupils from *'The Bible'* as a kind of *divertissement*. Perhaps for a few of the brightest girls, she might even help them to *'read and write'* out of lace school hours. In contrast most boys left the lace schools at nine or ten years of age to work on the land and frequently could not read or write as their wives could.

The countryside offered many opportunities to create intricate and beautiful designs. Lace makers had only to look around their cottage gardens to be inspired to make *'The Pea', 'The Bean', 'The Acorn' and 'The Spider' – and could draw on delightful subjects such as 'Pheasant's Eye' and 'Lucky Horseshoes'.*

An old Buckingham lace maker left us a fascinating story about the design of lace:

"On winter morns, when the hoar frost was thick upon the ground, my grandmother told me that her grandmother used to go, in company with the village folk, and draw the frosted cobwebs, trees, leaves and ferns in the fields and woods and return home and make new lace designs."

A favourite pattern, frequently taught to children beginning to make lace, was *'The Sheep's Head'* which really *is* like a sheep's head if you look at it quickly. When my sister and I were about seven and eight years old my Aunt taught us to do this as our first pattern working on the principle that if you could do that one you could do many of the simpler Bucks Point patterns as it contained most of the stitches in general use.

It is not difficult to imagine how a child would quickly learn to hate this pattern, struggling hard to work quickly and correctly, but inevitably making mistakes and being admonished by the teacher,

"SO DOO IT AGAIN."

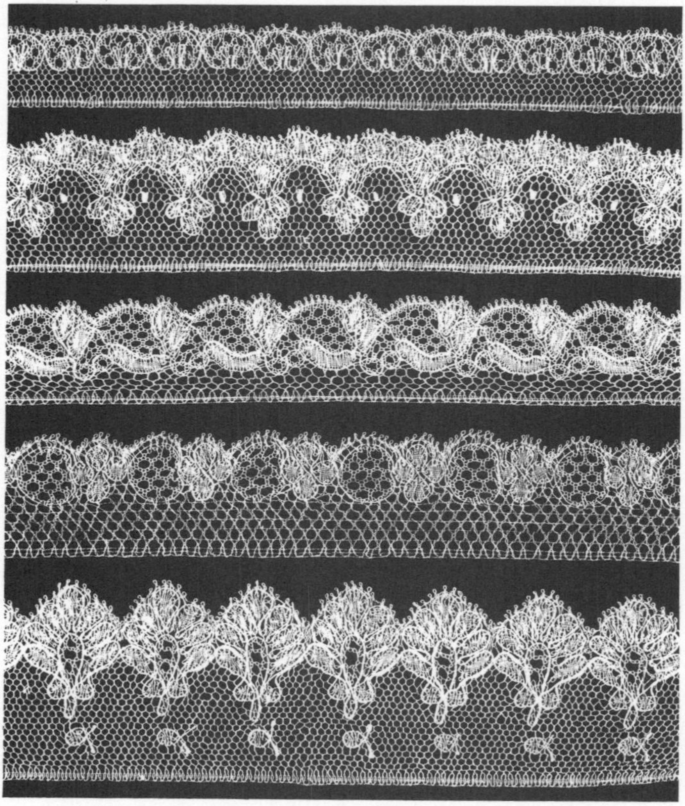

12

A Rich Heritage

It is not surprising that lace making was duly recorded by the poets of the day. Shakespeare, on his way to London from Stratford upon Avon, is reputed to have stopped at the village of Grendon Underwood, near to Waddesdon, as he travelled through Bucks. In his play, *'Twelfth Night'*, he has the Duke in ACT II SCENE IV say:

"The spinsters and the knitters in the sun And the free maids that weave their thread with bones."

In Shakespeare's day *'spinners'* were termed *'spinsters'* – he did not mean unmarried ladies!

Indeed, the making of lace in country cottages was well established as an industry during the reign of Queen Elizabeth. Even prior to this, legend would have us believe that when Henry VIII retired his Queen Katherine of Aragon to Ampthill in Bedfordshire, she taught the local people to make lace. Certainly she was an accomplished needlewoman, perhaps of embroidery or needle lace, but we are left with Katherine of Aragon patterns and *'Kat stitch ground'* to perpetuate the legend.

The same unhappy Queen had a little rhyme which was sung about her:

"I had a little nut tree, nothing would it bear
But a silver nutmeg and a golden pear
The King of Spain's daughter came to visit me
And all for the sake of my little nut tree."

Once you understand a little about lace making in the old days, you will also understand the message:

the *'little nut tree'* is the *'horse'* or *'stand'*, made of hazel branches on which the lace pillow rests;

the *'silver nutmeg'* was a small, silvery nutmeg shaped pincushion positioned at the side of the pillow;

the *'golden pear'* should, in fact, be spelled *'pair'* because it refers to the pair of golden pins that were once used at the foot (the straight plainer edge) of the lace.

Over the centuries, the prosperity of the lace industry has waxed and waned according to the dictates of fashion. Paintings by Old Masters show the Royalty and nobility of Europe positively decked in lace.

Queen Elizabeth, bedecked in fine lace

It is said that the reign of Charles II was the age of the lace collar and that of James II the age of the lace cravat. Discarding their own hair, men had taken to flowing wigs with long curls that completely hid the greater part of the collar, which, in consequence, gave place to the cravat. A lace cravat is still worn today as part of the ceremonial dress of High Court Judges and the Moderator of the Church of Scotland.

In 1688, when William III came to England to oust James II, he had many Huguenots amongst his troops. The change in Government apparently also brought a change in fashion. The lace cravat gave way to another neckcloth, the *'Steinkirk'*, an outcome of the battle of that name which took place in 1692. The French officers, not having time to arrange their cravats, knotted them hastily and drew them through a buttonhole and so, historians of fashion would have us believe, the tie was born.

During the reign of Queen Anne, lace *'jabots'*, or shirt frills, became the mode (for men of course), as well as *'weeping ruffles'*, or cuffs, that fell over the hands. Queens and Empresses had gowns made entirely of lace and their Bishops and Cardinals from the Church of Rome, liked to wear lace on their vestments as well as using it to adorn their altars.

But times were changing and, with the advent of a larger professional and middle class, ladies outside Court circles wanted to wear lace. Their men folk too also enjoyed being similarly adorned, but the lace worn now was narrower and more adaptable. Royalty, however, still wore lace and, at the time of her death, Queen Victoria's lace collection was said to be valued at £76,000 or at today's price, over a million pounds.

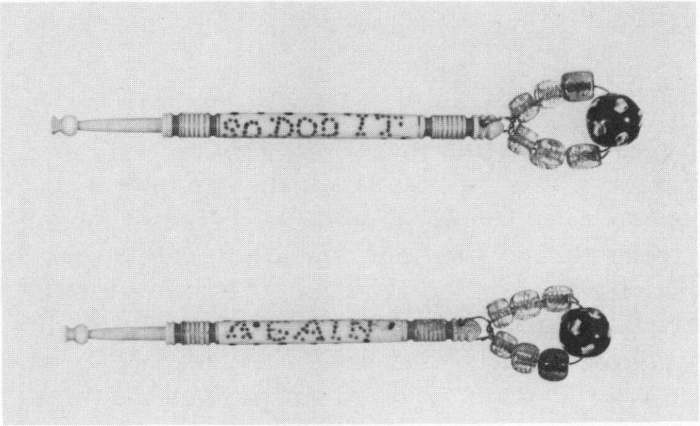

Changing Times

When the *'cottage lace industry'* was at its height, it was the custom for the lace buyers to go once a week to sell their wares in the lace markets at the *'George Inn'* and the *'Bull and Mouth'* in Aldersgate, London. Having sold their lace, they would return with stocks of thread which they gave out to their *'work women'* to make up. In this way, the cottagers did not have to buy the thread, they only worked it and were paid for their labours.

It is believed that around the year 1800, some 150,000 people were employed in the hand-made lace industry. This would have included the actual lace makers, the designers, the agents, the buyers, as well as all the *'middle men'* who made considerable profits. In contrast, at this same time only 15,000 were employed in the Nottingham area in the emerging machine lace industry. It was partly

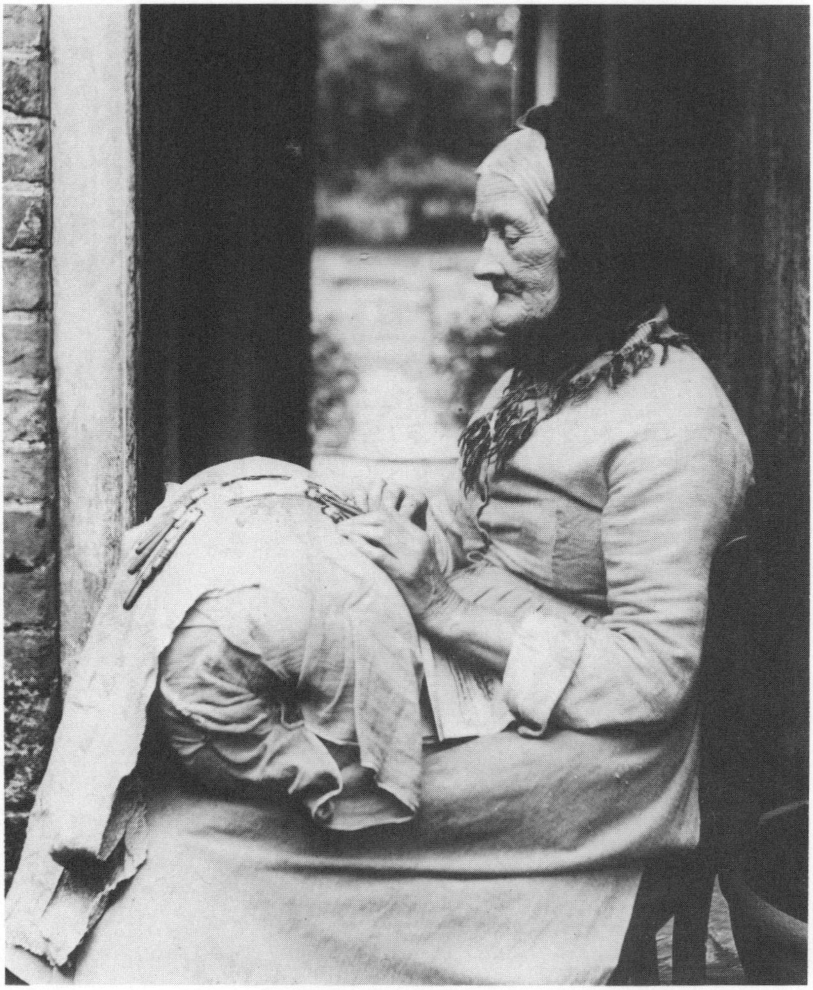

A lace maker outside her cottage in South Buckinghamshire

as a result of the introduction of wide machine-made lace in the early 1800s, that some of the Buckinghamshire lace makers began making narrow baby lace, chiefly used for trimming babies' caps and bonnets.

John Millward of Olney became famous for his *'rounds'* and *'crowns'* for babies' caps and a great number were exported to America until the Civil War closed this particular market.

During the 1850s when *Maltese Lace* designs were introduced in the area, they were originally known as *Bucks Maltese* but today are more generally known as *Bedfordshire*. The success of this new type of lace compared with the fine *Bucks Point* was due to the fact that it was not easily copied by the machines and was much more suitable for use on household linens, a new fashion in Victorian times.

By the end of the century, the quality of lace had so deteriorated that the North Bucks Lace Association was founded in 1897, with Queen Victoria as its Patron:

"to preserve and renew the best old designs, to discourage and stamp out as far as possible vulgar and degenerate forms of lace, to ensure the use of proper materials, and last, not least, to facilitate the sale of the lace direct from the workers to the purchaser, thus securing to the workers an adequate return for skilled labour, and saving the large profits made in all trade by the middlemen."

Waddesdon itself was also undergoing a dramatic change. In 1874 the whole life of the village changed when The Duke of Marlborough sold it (*'lock, stock and barrel'*, as the saying goes), to Baron Ferdinand de Rothschild who then began the building of The Manor. Hundreds of workers of all sorts came to the village bringing trade and a newfound prosperity.

Elsie Turnham's father, Henry Turnham, was the proprietor of The Marlborough Arms and Elsie was the eldest of his five children. The Baron had the old inn pulled down and replaced with a hotel, The Five Arrows, and the Turnham family were duly installed. The Hotel was very different from the old village inn. It had many bedrooms and served to accommodate artists, librarians and experts from all walks of life who gave their advice or expertise concerning the building and maintenance of The Manor and its contents. These artistic *'experts'* were not able to stay at The Manor: as they were not *gentry* (class-distinction was more strict in those days than it is today), nor could they be classed as servants to live in the servants' hall.

Surrounded by *'artists'* and artistic things all her life, it was only natural that Elsie Turnham would be interested in the beautiful local lace that is the nucleus of her collection. The decline and eventual death of the industry was gradual and could be attributed to many things – changes in fashion, the almost complete take-over by machine-made lace and the changes of life-style of the women in the country. Also in 1871, the Education Act came into force and with the introduction of compulsory education the village lace schools came to an end. By 1900 the cottage industry was virtually finished, having enjoyed a life of well over 300 years.

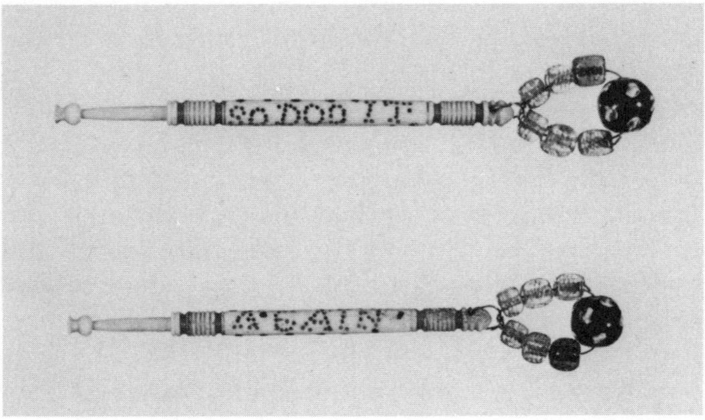

The 'new' Five Arrows hotel, soon after completion

A Collector of Lace

ELSIE TURNHAM was growing up in Waddesdon at the time of the death of the cottage industry. As a very young girl, she would see a few old ladies of the village sitting outside their cottages making lace.

Years later, Elsie Turnham recalled her own first experiences of lace making:

"In 1894, when I was nine years old, the village seamstress came to my mother and asked for the lace to put round the pinafores she was making for my sister and I. Mother told me to go over to Mrs Benjamin Marlow's house and see if it was done. I found her working at her pillow and can see myself standing there and saying very wistfully:

'Oh Mrs Marlow, I would love to make lace like that' *and her gruff reply,*
'Get yerself a pillar and bobbins and I'll soon larn yer'."

Elizabeth Rolfe, a Waddesdon lace maker

In later years she was quite willing to teach anyone who wanted to learn. But of course she used *'the method'* which had been used to teach her, a type of *'rule of thumb'*, no diagrams or explanation, just *'DOO IT'* or, more likely, *'DOO IT AGAIN'*.

During the years up to the Great War, it was customary for daughters who had married and gone away from the village to return to *'clear out'* the cottage when an old lace maker died. The advice of neighbours would be to:

"take all the lace and bobbins to Miss Turnham at The Five Arrows. She collects that sort of thing."

The chances were, they would get a pint of beer or payment if they asked for it. The alternative would have been the trouble of burning it or, during the summer, throwing it under cover of darkness into one of the Rothschild's plantations. As the collection built up, wherever she went she would be on the look-out for new items to add to her collection. During this time no one else appeared to be the least bit interested in lace which had only been made in the cottages of the agricultural workers. We must all of us be eternally grateful that one person in Bucks gave shelter to the tools of the trade and the bits and pieces left by the old lace makers in their cottages. There are, of course, beautiful specimens of *Bucks Point Lace* in many museums, but these pieces would have been the property of, and have been worn by, the wealthy.

Nothing was too *'poor'* or *'simple'* for Elsie Turnham to collect. She took in everything that was brought to her, including patterns (known as prickings), by the hundreds. Many of these were *'one off'* designs – the jealously guarded secrets of a particular family and handed down from one generation to another. The richness of some of these old patterns serves as inspiration for both working and designing today. How much nicer to use an *old* pattern than make up a *modern* one.

Elsie Turnham's parents retired to a small house in Aylesbury in the 1920s and she moved with them. When eventually she was on her own she had to manage on a very small income of diminishing dividends. However, survive she did and was frequently to be seen in the small, local towns of Buckingham, Winslow, Stony Stratford, Princes Risborough, Thame, etc., scouring the market stalls and antique shops for bobbins to add to her collection. There must have been times when she was hard-pressed to find even a few spare pennies to acquire an unusual or particularly fine specimen of a bobbin. Amongst her papers are many references to her delight at receiving gifts of unusual bobbins, or finding a bargain on a market stall.

Upon her death in 1953, her collection of lace was inherited by my mother who left it to my sister and I. We have tried to preserve it and to extend it, for the benefit of future generations of lace makers.

The Lace in the Collection

AMONGST the lace in the collection are several *'hanks'* of *Bucks Point Lace* ready for the lace buyers to collect. These are neatly sewn together in a hank six yards long, with a small strip of coloured paper in the middle to highlight the pattern. I have never seen lace anywhere else *'ready for the market'* and can only assume these hanks had not been sold and came from cottages in Waddesdon. Perhaps when an old lace makers' bits and pieces were being cleared out, these were taken to The Five Arrows rather than being disposed of as worthless. I remember my Aunt saying that all the old lace makers she knew only ever made lace by the yard on a bolster pillow. They never made fancy bits and never did corners.

It is not known where all the small lace items in the collection came from, but I feel they would have been gifts. I remember my Aunt saying many times that after giving talks to ladies' organisations she would be sent pieces of lace, the doner often inferring it would be *'given a good home'*. Every Wednesday and Saturday, from the late 1930s till the time of her death, Elsie Turnham would sit in The County Museum at Aylesbury making lace on a pillow she kept there for the purpose. She had some of her special bobbins on the pillow to show the interested visitors just how skilled the old bobbin makers were.

There are many items of interest in the collection for the needlewoman – embroidery done by my Mother, crochet work done by my Grandmother – but who embroidered the pictures or worked the samplers, no one knows.

Elsie Turnham collected all forms of lace made with bobbins: with a needle, a crochet hook, a tatting shuttle, knitting needles etc. She preserved and treasured it all.

During my own travels, I have bought bobbin lace in Romania, Malta, Ceylon, Singapore and Hong Kong and needle made lace in Cyprus, Jerusalem, The Philippines, to name but a few and examples of these are now in the collection.

Bobbins

Elsie Turnham's Collection of lace bobbins is extremely comprehensive, ranging from the plain wooden bobbins of the working lace maker, to the elaborately decorated bone bobbins which are much sought after today. We are indebted to Christine and David Springett for their valuable work in identifying and organising the bobbins on display in the exhibition.

The earliest bobbins used by the cottage lace maker would have been made by husbands, sons, relations and friends. Most were *'whittled'* from fruit woods such as apple, pear, cherry and plum which gave a good close grained timber and were readily available in the villages. A considerable degree of skill could be achieved as shown in one example containing a miniature bobbin pierced with a loose ball. They were also carved in bone to

The Saunders Brothers, Waddesdon: turned wooden bobbins

record christenings, weddings, or even hangings and frequently as tokens of love.

Later full-time bobbin makers took advantage of the consumer market and the work of many of these are represented in the collection.

The Saunders Family, perhaps the most interesting bobbin-makers, because of their local connections, were the Waddesdon family of the Saunders brothers, who are mentioned by Thomas Wright. Richard and his brother Thomas, from nearby Quainton, with John and Jonah Saunders made a wide variety of bobbins and produced some unique bobbins in a style of decoration more commonly found in furniture. However they also made many bobbins inlaid with pewter in a wide variety of attractive and unusual styles.

The collection also comprises the work of many other bobbin-makers and it is fascinating to compare their different work and syles:

William *'bobbin'* **Brown**, 1793–1872, who lived at Cranfield, Bedfordshire, produced inscribed bobbins which show outstandingly neat lettering. In comparison, those made by his pupil, the son of a local pillow maker Arthur Wright, do not!

The Saunders Brothers, Waddesdon: turned wooden bobbins with peweter inlay

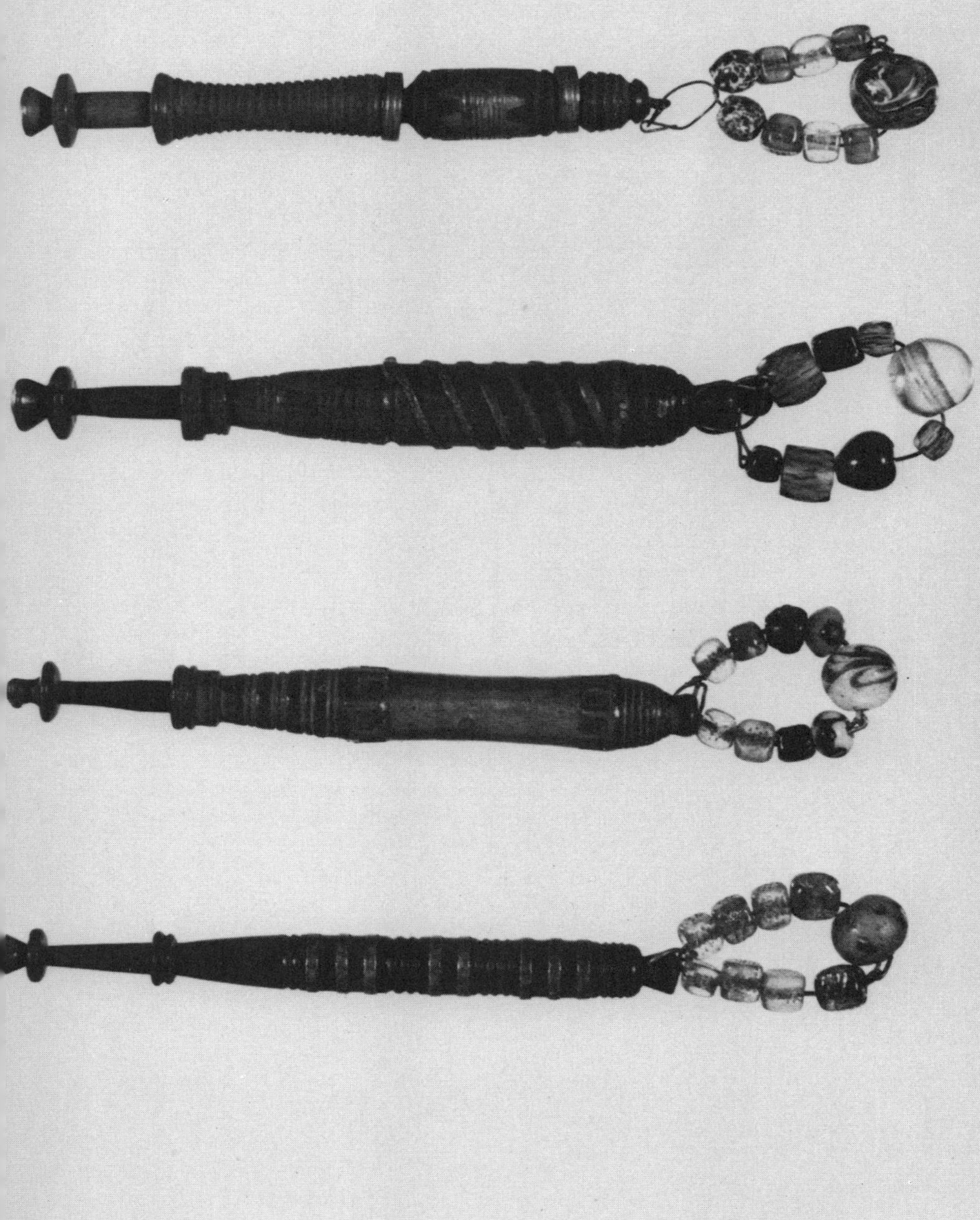

Jessie Compton, 1793–1856, who with his son James, 1824–1889, produced many bobbins over a period of 80 years. Yet they never described themselves as bobbin-makers, referring to themselves as *"Turners, Hawkers and Labourers."* The range and the changing styles of their work are particularly interesting as the changing styles reflect the shift from fine lace at the beginning of the century, to the coarser Bedfordshire/Maltese types introduced to compete with machine-made lace.

The Haskin Family: Joseph, 1779–1855, made the finest bobbins in the early 1800s, a tradition continued by his son David and his grandson Robert. Their work is also interesting as they made use of the new chemical dyes to create bright colours to add to the appearance of their bobbins.

Archibald Abbot, 1815–1885, was a furniture maker from Bedford, who probably made bobbins from his *'off-cuts'*. Thomas Wright records his fame as a maker of fine bobbins decorated with pewter butterflies and tigers.

Examples can also be seen of the work of lesser-known bobbin makers such as:

The **'Blunt-ended man'**, his work is identified because he gave little or no shaping at the tail-end

The Work of Other Bobbin Makers: from bottom to top – William 'bobbin' Brown – Jesse and James Compton – Joseph, David and Robert Haskin – Archibald Abbott – The 'blunt-ended man' – The 'bitted man' – The 'rotten pewter man'

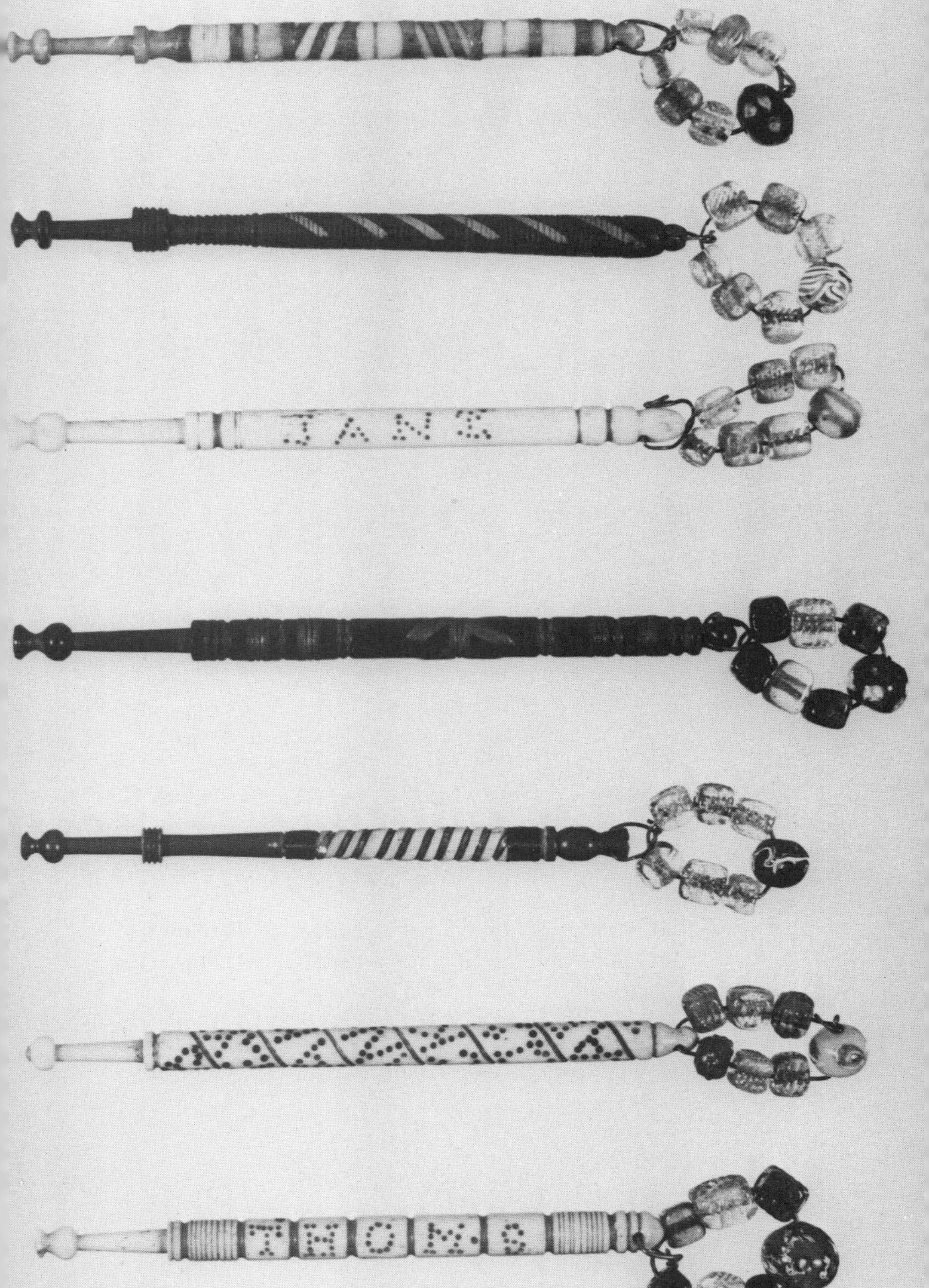
JANE

and also left a typically square shape to the head. In addition, his letters nearly always sloped upwards and he usually missed out the dots from the letters A and E.

The **'Bitted Man'**, an unknown maker, working in the early 1800s, he produced *'Bitted'* bobbins of outstanding quality and design. These were inlayed with woods of a contrasting colour into the shank to form initials.

The **'Rotten Pewter Man'**, who produced bobbins with highly intricate pewter inlays many of which suffered a high degree of corrosion.

Many of the old bobbins collected by Elsie Turnham bear inscriptions, most commonly a person's name, but sometimes a token of love such as:

MARRY ME
LOVE IS SHARP TO FEAL THE SMART
KISS ME QUIK MY MOM IS COMING
VALENTINE
I LOVE THEM THAT LOVE M 1843
MARRY BUT DONT TARRY
CONSTANT PROVE TO ME MY LOVE
LOVE ALL
NEVER GO COURTING TO LACES (two lasses) AT ONCE

However the bobbins in the collection also contain a wide range of other inscriptions including texts from the scripture, a line from a song, a moral sentence, as well as recording elections, marriages, hangings, births and deaths.

Many of the bobbins are elaborately decorated with pewter (made from discarded tableware or stolen beer tankards!) and have acquired special names over the years:

BUTTERFLY OR BEDFORD 'FLY
TIGERS (with stripes)
LEOPARDS (with spots)

One of the examples of a *'leopard bobbin'* has raised spots and these acquired a reputation over the years of protecting the lace maker from arthritis and rheumatism.

There are many fine examples of elaborately carved and decorated bone bobbins such as:

PIERCED MOTHER AND BABES
CHURCH WINDOWS
JACK IN A BOX

There are also fine examples of exquisitely beaded and wired bobbins which prove that *'all that glistens is not gold'*. Although brass wire may shine like gold, it is the result of continuous handling by the lace maker who has *'polishing hands'*.

Tinsell was also used to create colourful or striking decoration and such bobbins frequently acquired the name *'fairings'*, recalling the bright glittery objects which were associated with the travelling fairs.

One of the most attractive aspects of the collection is the range of old beads on the Jingles or Spangles which prevented the bobbin rolling on the pillow and added tension to the thread. Lace makers used a wide variety of items to achieve this and examples can be seen of coins, buttons, seeds, nuts, shells and charms to this end, but the glass beads were the most common and most attractive to the eye.

My favourite bobbin in the collection is inscribed, *"SO DOO IT AGAIN."* What was it that someone was entreated to do again ? Was it a small girl being bounced on her father's knee who screamed with delight *"SO DOO IT AGAIN"*; or the bashful young lady who was kissed by her first suitor and, enjoying it, asked him to *"SO DOO IT AGAIN"*; or the young wife, presenting her husband with a son and heir, being asked *"SO DOO IT AGAIN?"* It is a request that is full of wonder and speculation, perhaps an order to repeat some task properly, but more intriguing to think it was an entreaty to repeat something nice.

Some finely decorated bobbins from the Elsie Turnham Collection: from bottom to top – Pierced 'Mother and Babe' 3-decker by Joseph Haskins – Tinselled 'Mother and Babe' probably by David Haskins – A rare bobbin with four beads on shaft – A finely beaded bobbin – A pierced 'Church Window' – A 'Jack in a Box' with a miniature bobbin inside – A 'fairings' – A 'Wired bobbin'

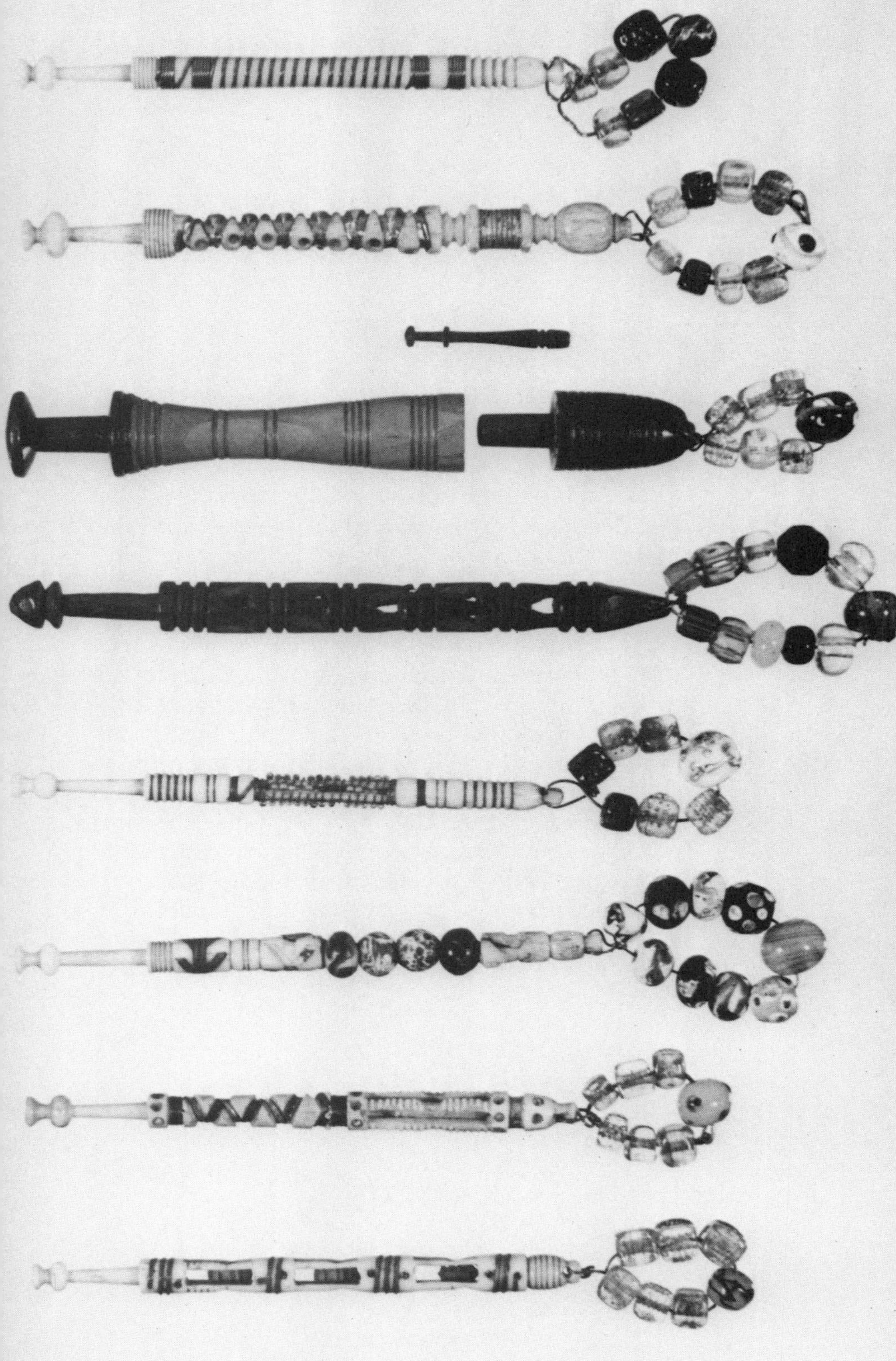

Today's Lace Makers

It is thought that the popularity of pillow lace making today owes a tremendous debt to the fact that hundreds and thousands of ladies are finding that they have time on their hands and want to *'make something'*. Many were just grown up when the War broke out in 1939, so it meant war work, then marriage and children, then work again to gain a better life for their children and some little extras. Their houses were all labour saving, all push buttons, but still with no spare time to sew clothes or knit jumpers and anyway it was cheaper to buy *'ready mades'*. They have never had the time or opportunity to make some thing frivolous with their hands. Pillow lace fulfils this longing.

To sit at one's pillow takes a certain amount of concentration, but not too much so that it becomes a chore. On the other hand, it is repetative and

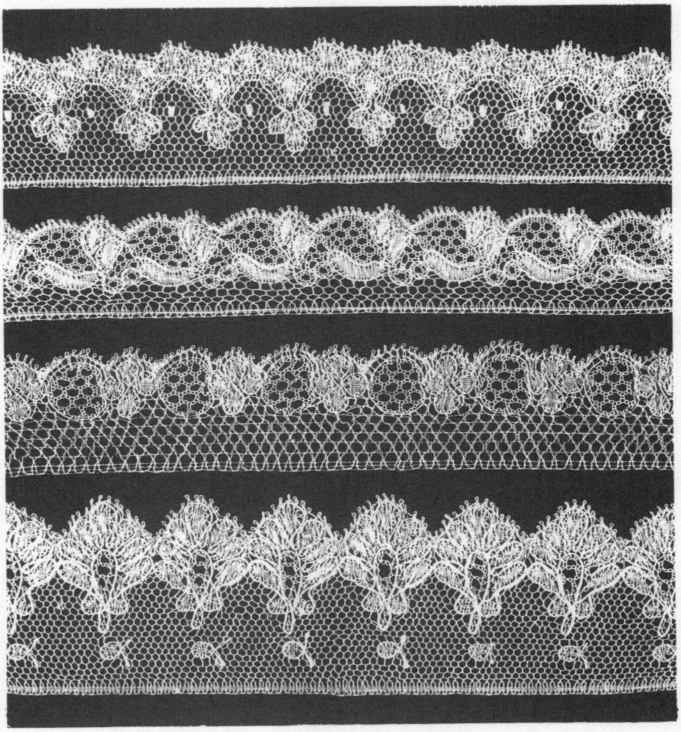

follows a pattern, so its not an insurmountable problem to work out. It is therapeutic and a delightful occupation, a relaxation that has no equal and its not therefore surprising that the ladies of today have sought out the delights of this old craft and *"SO DOO IT AGAIN."*

But perhaps when they do, they will recall the old working lace makers of Buckinghamshire and the old Bucks rhyme which was found on a Christmas card that had been sent to Elsie:

"Copses and woods and cornfields mellow
Elm trees tall, green, gold and yellow
Gardens and orchards folding around
Thatched cottages in ancient grounds.

This is the country known as Bucks
T'is noted for its Aylesbury ducks
Three poets and great statesmen four
It's lace is famous the world o'er.

In such a lovely countryside
The craftsmen thrive well satisfied
Churches and buildings testify
To man's great skill in days gone by.

Pleasant agricultural scenes
Lush country and slow flowing streams
In fields where raged the bloody battle
Contentedly now graze fat cattle.

May factories long be kept at bay
Farms grow more prosperous day by day
And Bucks continue to deserve
The heart of England to preserve."